A Visit to The Farm

Revised Edition

Blake A Hoena

a Capstone company — publishers for children

Raintree is an imprint of Capstone Global Library Limited, a company incorporated in England and Wales having its registered office at 264 Banbury Road, Oxford, OX2 7DY – Registered company number: 6695582

www.raintree.co.uk
myorders@raintree.co.uk

Text © Capstone Global Library Limited 2018

Editorial credits
Sarah Bennett, designer; Tracy Cummins, media researcher; Laura Manthe, production specialist

Acknowledgements
We would like to thank the following for permission to reproduce photographs: Alamy: Rafael Ben-Ari, 7; Capstone Press: Gary Sundermeyer, 9, 13, 15, 17, 19; iStockphoto: mixetto, 21; Shutterstock: amirage, Design Element, Janis Apels, 11, melissaf84, Cover Background, 5, withGod, Cover Left

Printed and bound in India

ISBN 978 1 4747 5632 7
22 21 20 19 18
10 9 8 7 6 5 4 3 2 1

British Library Cataloguing in Publication Data
A full catalogue record for this book is available from the British Library.

Every effort has been made to contact copyright holders of material reproduced in this book. Any omissions will be rectified in subsequent printings if notice is given to the publisher.

All the Internet addresses (URLs) given in this book were valid at the time of going to press. However, due to the dynamic nature of the Internet, some addresses may have changed, or sites may have changed or ceased to exist since publication. While the author and publisher regret any inconvenience this may cause readers, no responsibility for any such changes can be accepted by either the author or the publisher.

Contents

The farm

A farm is a fun place to visit.
Farms have buildings, fields
and animals.

5

Farm buildings

Barns are large buildings where animals live. Barns also hold crops and equipment. Farmers milk cows in barns.

Grain bins hold food that farm animals eat. Bins are round and wide.

Farm animals

Chickens look for food
around the farm.
They peck at the ground.

Sheep graze.
They eat the grass
in a pasture.

13

Pigs stay in their pens.

Pigs snort and squeal.

Fields and crops

Farmers use tractors

in their fields.

Tractors pull

heavy machinery.

Farmers drive combines.

Combines help farmers pick

or harvest crops in autumn.

A farm is an important place.

The food people and animals eat

comes from a farm.

Glossary

barn building where animals, crops and equipment are kept

combine powerful vehicle that picks or harvests crops when they are finished growing in a field

field area of land used for growing crops

graze eat grass that is growing in a field or pasture

pasture land that animals use to graze

tractor powerful vehicle that has large wheels; tractors pull farm machinery, trailers and heavy loads

Read more

Books

On the Farm (Young Starters) Rod Campbell, (Macmillan Children's Books, 2017)

Farmer (People Who Help Us) Rebecca Hunter, (Tulip Books Ltd., 2014)

On a Farm (Penguin Young Readers - Level One) Alexa Andrews, (Penguin, 2013)

Websites

www.bbc.co.uk/cbeebies/shows/down-on-the-farm
Watch a fun children's show all about the farm, you'll find some fun games to play too.

www.activityvillage.co.uk/farm-animals
Discover lots of exciting activities and crafts to do with the farm at this website.

Comprehension questions

1. Why are barns important on a farm?

2. Describe one or two jobs a farmer does on a farm.

3. Would you like to visit a farm? Why or why not?

Index